The <u>Cold</u> Towing

Frozen blue-white bean fields
no crows, no deer
no shadows
yet all is in shadow
this dawn in Indiana
bare trees with stiff
fingers caught in misty hair nets
the thermometer reads minus 8,
hint of sunlight orange-tinged
white jet tails like wisps
of breath hung high in the air
where something was —

nothing moves
save me
at 80 mph
alone on I-90 de-iced asphalt
driving into sunrise
with ten-thousand days in tow.

POSTCARDS TO JACK

poems and haibun
from
the road

Albert DeGenova

Redbee Editions
an imprint of Argus House Press
Second Expanded Edition
2017

First Edition 2010 Naked Mannekin
Design and artwork by Matthew S. Barton

Second Edition 2017 Redbee Editions
an imprint of Argus House Press

ISBN 978-1-64136-125-5

dedicated to

NORBERT BLEI

writer
mentor and friend

ACKNOWLEDGEMENTS

"Time to Go" and "Unveiled," *Open: Journal of Arts and Letters* (online: http://ojalart.com/), November 2017

"Postcard from Washington Island" and "On Green Bay," *Soundings* anthology of Door County (Wisc.) poetry, Carravagio Press, May 2015

"Backdoor Postcard" (first place) and "Postcard from Compartment 58" (fourth place), Flashquake.org (print and online), Haibun Contest, May 2011

"Tourist," *Bigger Than They Appear* anthology of short poems, Accents Publishing, June 2011

" Postcard from Milan," *Contemporary Haibun Vol. 12*, Red Moon Press, April 2011

"Postcard from Washington Island" and "Postcard from Berlin," *Contemporary Haibun Online*, December 2010

"Postcard from Ixtapa" and "Postcard from NYC," *Haibun Today*, September 2010

"Condemned," BloodLotus, online journal, July 2010

"Postcard from Seattle," *Haibun Today*, March 2010

"Postcard from Prague," *Modern Haibun and Tanka Prose*, December 2009

"Postcard from Napoli," *Haibun Today*, October 2009

" Drink It Like Water," *After Hours,* Summer 2009

TABLE OF CONTENTS

cold rain, sleepless—
beard grows
whisker by whisker

I read you Jack, Loud but not so clear anymore – you
put the American landscape into words, claimed it as
your own. But what did you leave for me in this new
century? On your quest for "it" – no mind –
transcendence – leaving the post-bomb generation
madness behind – as Charlie Parker would close his
eyes and blow himself into the shelter of his crazy alto
saxophone – Jazz man! you blew yourself into the
pages of your notebooks and became the asphalt of
sad Rt. 66, the gravel voice of all-night diners, the
breath of the hungry wind that blows from San
Francisco to New York to Tangiers. You blew your
words and brains out with a bottle of cheap wine –
where is "it" at now, Old Angel Midnight?

I'm drowning in this new century, Jack – electricity
and plastic and Wi-Fi nights of virtual conversation
 – programmed thinking, programmed wars,
programmed music, programmed religion. I'm thirsty
for a glass of Grandpa's dago red – Miles is in the sky –
my bed was so cold this morning, the thermostat lost
its memory – cell phone rings and no one is there, I'm
out of signal bars. Gotta go, gotta go, gotta go,
we're all gonna fuckin' explode!

LONESOME TRAVELER

Kerouac, you have a way with "sad" –
sad cracked hands of all-night diners,
sad gravel under shapeless shoes,
sad waning moon of November roads.

Sentimental sadness, familiar
sadness, old friend
sad Jack, tell me if
sad tastes like black dust to you
if it smells like burning leaves,
tell me it is more than easy metaphor
'cuz I can taste it on my breakfast toast.

Such a small word for a poet
so much smaller than love
the distillate of love –
grand love that inspires
yet lives and dies
in three breaths –
sad is old as coal
and deep in veins
reaching to our core, old friend,
the sad eternal core.

Drink that last shot down, buddy,
it's a long cold walk to the diner.

white gull, dark wind
driftwood against steel pier

POSTCARD FROM KEY WEST

Woman with Barbie doll hair plays bongos – rhythms
without tempo – locks the small drums between her
legs like a Latin lover – her blind eye looks away, the
other glares a piercing stare – "illusion delusion,
allusion to a dream" she chants at vacationers who
rush to the end of the pier – they raise plastic cups,
Rum Punch and Margaritas to celebrate the daily
Sunset Festival – she raises her empty tip jar, toasting
her audience – "Cuba is only 90 miles away, you can
swim it," she urges.

DeeDee? is that her
walking across a lawn, someone's lawn,
I know she lives here
          somewhere,
is it on this
Orlando street?
heart heavy
in heavy Florida air
how did I ever misplace her...DeeDee gone gone gone.

No one home at the Kerouac Cottage
Jack Jack
beautiful Jack
1958 Jack
under this tree
rucksack generation
Dharma Bums fell onto the page.
Sitting lotus position under this tree – the moss
hanging tropical –
you told the story
of California mountains
and poets and Buddha – all
so far away from this tree, this Florida swamp.

searching shadows for an outstretched hand
she is not here
you are not here
that is not her voice –
echoes of children bouncing balls.

I search for you Jack
I search for your tree
the sound of your typewriter
    hanging from the limbs,
pages
  unrolling from the moss –
write her into this scene Jack
I need you to do it for me Jack –
DeeDee on the porch with a pitcher of iced tea.

Jack Jack
beautiful Jack
your inspiration laps against the shore
your joy falls drunk against the peeling white cottage
your finger is in my back digging a trench to my heart
your cottage is no fountain of truth
the passenger seat is empty

Jack! DeeDee!
my saxophone lays silent in an Orlando hotel
my love hides under the keys
my poems scatter like rabbits in be-bop rhythm.

Run Jack! Hide Jack!
The swamp will swallow you
it digests my DeeDee like so much reedy regret
my saxophone suffocates—
my pen
falls out of my hand.

LOS ABUELOS de SAN JUAN

Under the amber lights of Saturday night,
plantains, sugar cane and coffee on the wind,
viejos gather in the plaza by the bay,
and in a tight ring of folding chairs the *antigua* sing

folk songs. With their guitars, stiff-legged men
strum like teenagers – with their *cabassas*
and *maracas* the gathering crowd shakes the rhythm,
with *bongos* and *cajones* they feel

the time of their ancestors.
One dark woman in pink ruffles scratches music
on her guiro, another in a wheelchair wears
a black derby and jangles her tambourine.

In unison these smiling women with
faces of Africa and Spain and mountain Indians,
faces framed with dangling earrings
and pearl beads, sing in Caribbean Spanish

no, es no es de aqui
of lost loves and hard lives in lost centuries,
todos junto their matronly hips
sway to the *clave*, the ringing clink

clink   clink-clink
of two wooden sticks calls the dance,
tells their sandaled feet where
to move, holds the song in its pace.

gull to piling
skateboard to boardwalk
sunset

POSTCARD FROM SEATTLE

Street dark, almost deserted at Pike's Place Market,
I see your shadow Kerouac, listening to a bearded
grunge guitar player with two violinists in summer tank
tops and long gauze skirts – the girls black-soled
barefoot, hair in uncombed blond curls and waves.
They play folk-rock ballads on the sidewalk in front of a
closed and dark jazz café – the tourists all gone.

UNVEILED

ing Chicago to Seattle, at the airport gate, a glaring anachronism,
in traditional habit sits talking on her cell phone, scrolling down the screen of her
 – she walks behind me as we board, she sits in the window seat next to me –

nic is deep blue linen, the veil, wimple and un-starched scapular are white poplin –
her is a subtle musty scent of underarm – in her mid-thirties, soft featured,
adorned prettiness. I notice she slips off her shoes. When not reading, she holds

f, arms crossed hugging her torso – when reading, her free hand strokes wispy
e hair on the wrist of her book hand, or runs a finger along the strong line of her jaw –
reading a book entitled "The Mass" but puts it aside for the airline magazine. I

ler her life without touch, Vestal virgin, a vocation, a calling – I fall
. The rosary attached to her belt fills the space between us. When I wake, she
ep, her face turned toward the window, the sun is bright, we are above the clouds –

rk-hosed toes of her left foot rest on the top of my sandaled right foot – her
osed toes open and close as if barefoot on a white flokati rug – I am paralyzed,
city running up my leg.

CONDEMNED

At a ranch in the dark hills outside of Las Vegas
girls lined-up in their tattoos and laces –
one whispered between giggles, *I always get the short ones.*
Later at the $4.99 buffet of the Seven Deadlies
we drank gasoline and smoked fat cigars
all for one and one for all musketeers
we called that years-ago night our *Original.*

Tonight Kentucky wives kick off their shoes
        and wiggle their painted toes.
I sing Dr. John's prescription
        for love and happiness
and me tokin' from a glass pipe
        drinkin' warm bourbon –
It's a good thing we didn't have one more
        she says, *leave the lights on*
I've never seen you before.

Enjoy my magic carpet ride little one, you
you with your thumb up.

SHIVER

Tall window
Las Vegas neon rainbow far below
glowing eyes that might be watching
pull her.

Dark nipple touches cold glass.

Shiver
that melts the moon
the staring neon eyes
the cresting sea
inside
her.

dark doorway
greasy brown bag
eating alone

POSTCARD FROM NYC

One hundred degrees today, Manhattan is a
clay oven – through the café window I watch
women rushing passed in summer attire, bare
shoulders and legs glistening, the warm
breeze lingering under their skirts – inside,
a cheap steak and dry Malbec, an expensive
cigar and a leather couch, Jack Daniels neat,
wood paneling, jazz trio in a corner next to the
bar – piano man oblivious to all except the
long-legged waitress, the black angel smiling,
the cool air-conditioned midnight.

rain on concrete
black loafers and red high heels
midnight

POSTCARD FROM MILAN

Just arrived, 10 pm, searching alone for city-center
Duomo and Metro stops – graffiti everywhere – walk
and walk saying street names out loud, Italian accented,
so I can find my way back to my little one-star hotel –
stop for espresso and pastry at a street vendor, check
out Duomo, hundreds of carved spire fingers all
reaching to heaven in sad earthly fashion – so many
people, more and more as it gets later and later, now
midnight, all ages – stop to buy Italian Toscano brand
cigars, smoke, remember my great-grandfather
chewing unlit black butt – along narrow street back to
hotel undistinguished facades hide luxurious garden
courtyards – I spy one of these courtyards as a couple
kisses goodnight at a giant half-opened door – couples
make-out in cars, this wonderful spring! oh, the kissing
nature of this city! oh, the long-nosed face of Italy! –
the language I can't understand surrounds me,
awakens my childhood, makes me smile in salty ocean
waves of Italian vowels – taste grandma's meatballs
on my 10-year-old tongue.

train fare and newspaper
plum orchard blossoms

POSTCARD FROM COMPARTMENT 58

Train Rome to Naples, countryside covered in
grapevines, orchards planted in careful rows, tomatoes
already sprouting—the fields are planted around, along
the hills, the sturdy thick farmers walk the hard ancient
paths—cows and goats know more than they say—soil
of these fields, layer after layer of fertile decay,
generation upon generation of bones, olive pits, and
grape stems—my peasant legs ache to walk these
terraced hills, the stamina of time and grandfathers'
DNA—sharing the compartment an older Italian couple
pours coffee from a thermos, fills water from a glass
bottle into small paper cups, a roll of paper towels for
wiping the man's sweating bald head—I can smell the
sweet juicy ripeness of the pear he slices with a
well-used pocketknife, the handle smooth and black.

cedar roots
in limestone bluffs
ten thousand winds

POSTCARD FROM NAPOLI

First view of the Mediterranean, walking the
Napolitain shore, entranced by the
fishermen—their dark suntanned skin
cracked like worn canvas or bark or the
seasoned hulls of their wooden boats—
bare hands are forever leather gloves—
folding, mending ancient nets—their boats
insignificant against the sea, mismatched
to the heavy loads they drag out of the
waves. Seaside café—I will eat fresh
succulent *pullipo*, octopus in oil, lemon,
and herbs.

Hands in the warm sea, Mediterranean sand
under my fingernails, lose my breath, heart
beats startled, unknown ghost or saint
drifts up behind me—I have been homesick
all of my life—this is where I want to die.

DRINK IT LIKE WATER

The fountain pen is
empty. Not the night
for poetry or postcards.
Under whose bed
did I leave my saxophone?

Leaning against a white stone
building in Florence, the rain
corrals me into a shrinking
dry spot – I smoke
the last cigar. Between which pages
of fiction did I leave
my worn passport?

Vacations are not the context
for questions. Naples
has a sticky handshake.
Layers of Rome linger
in clouds of ancient incense. Temples
and crosses and red wine flowing
from a brass tap in the wall –
you've got to drink it all, drink it
like water. The thirst, the thirst.

Who's your deity, Daddio?

BOHEMIAN SUNSET

Electric tram, steel wheels on steel track
glides into purple dusk
foggy silence
too tired to speak of where it's been.

A man walks an uphill path toward dinner
small child on his shoulders
sleeping
soft red cheek against Papa's head.

Rain falls like a Chopin melody
upon a black slate roof that listens
eyes closed
as a young couple embraces under its eave.

Small pensione, window full open
a man stands smoking a cigar
eyes blank
remembering a rowboat
floating aimlessly under Gothic cathedrals,
a riverside café, two glasses of red wine –
and Czech faces like wise poems in dusty jackets.

the crow doesn't caw
riding an updraft, alone
into the sun

POSTCARD FROM PRAGUE

Old Town Square built centuries before "jez" music
made its way out of Storyville whore houses – feel the
sultry steamy sentiments that surround New Orleans in
my mind as a band of street musicians play Dixieland
with a gravel-ly Bohemian accent in the center of the
square, cobblestones under feet, dumplings in bellies –
they overpower the Baroque melodies of a lonely boy
with his recorder who plays on a corner near a café
where Mozart finds his way through speakers defiantly
filling the spaces between breaths of the Satchmo-esque
trumpet – and all of this gets the old square's statues of
saints, and kings, and musicians, and artists, and
heroes closing their eyes, covering their ears – tourists
gather at the foot of the Clock Tower, everything stops
on the hour, each hour, when the clock performs its
magical mechanical dance – its centuries-old dance,
bells chiming the irony of time – as in the Gothic torture
museum at the foot of a sleeping castle, in the shadows
of a palace and cathedral that cast their lofty attitude
above the city, as in Kafka's words, in the gypsy violins
– the soul survives.

THE DANCE

This is not your hand not your hair
not your head against my shoulder –
you are four thousand miles away

and I am here dancing with Elke
this sweet woman who does not
long for my smile, nor I
for her spring water blue eyes – yet we dance
like lovers -- to whispers
and titters
of colleagues who elbow
and nod
        at us
            dancing
thigh to thigh
fingers to fingers—
but our eyes
        our eyes only brush in passing
the slight touch of understanding.

Is that you
in the air
in the red and orange flashing lights?
your sweat?
your perfume?
Dizzy with dancing
        my pounding blood
tastes like the sea
on the back of your neck
thousands of miles
and days
from this dance
you and your
red dress...
        your brown eyes.

To her friend's question
What did he say to you?
Elke answers,
We had no need for words.

SUNSET ON THE DOME
(Cologne, Germany, October 26, 2002)

In the Dome Plaza skateboarders spin, curse, jump and
laugh over the crumbling crypt of a Roman governor –
museum remnant of a broken empire –

below the plaza, below these red bricks, the Philharmonic
can hear tourists with their cameras and shopping bags
walking on its roof

the cardinal who yearned to boast his church the biggest
tool of redemption smiles from his sarcophagus
for the clicking shutters, yet doesn't hear

the throng outside the chapel doors
Polizei on motorcycles, in green jumpsuits,
stone-faced, protecting their saints

fathers and sons shouting through megaphones
against this war, another war that worries the wind,
that blows in from somewhere beyond the *Rhein*

that builds around the spires – a tempest of dead Romans,
soldiers and whores panting,
fat old priests eating –

bombs will fall again, empires will fall again
and tourists, stepping over the rubble,
will gather broken bricks for souvenirs
again.

HISTORICAL VAULTS WITH IMPERIRAL DUNGE

(museum, Rothenburg, Germany)

Today I touch 400-year-old armor
survivor of the Thirty Years War,
run my hand over black-brown
metal ruffle of overlapping elbow protection –

memory flash of red
across the back of a black t-shirt
U.S. Marine Corps slogan in bold block letters
"Pain is weakness leaving the body" –

put my fingertips to scabby, crumbling
cloth, a glove that held a hand
whose mortal strength strained
to swing a broadsword –

look into the slim slot of your visor
how much of the battle could you see
and I remember San Francisco graffiti
"Stop praising the God of war!" spewed in spray paint.

Before the archer releases his bowstring
I kiss your cold breastplate

Bless you
tender empty soldier.

from the kettle's belly

screaming

before tea

POSTCARD FROM BERLIN

This city steals my stomach, block after block –
spiraling stairs, glass-domed Reichstadt haunted by
blonde-haired ghosts, black wings and swastikas, mirrored
axis of this spiral dream-vision illuminating the most
feared Parliament in Europe – bombed-out church hunched
like a crippled vet with a tin cup – Checkpoint Charlie
Museum, gray grained photos, people shot by countrymen,
a man left to bleed to death wrapped in barbed wire, dark
escape tunnels of *Bernauerstrasse* – I walk up open
stairways, down halls of a bombed-out no-façade building
where homeless artists have made beds and studios for 40
years, sold sketches on brown paper bags (50
DeutschMarks), hawked beer and schnapps from a
makeshift broken-plank bar.

*It was not sex, it was not joy, it was something else,
something I cannot say – when the Wall came down,*
says Jergen, 60-year-old tour guide Berliner, his teeth
knocked out in an East Berlin prison – as a young student,
reported for something said in a café over cold coffee,
among friends. I buy a cement chip of the Wall with
authentic, they say, hints of graffiti paint...to remember
Jerg and his thin hippie beard.

DEFINING "PEACE"
AT A FESTIVAL OF THE SAME NAME

Peace echoed like too much Dr. Seuss,
like the graying poet, knobby white-kneed
reading to almost no one –
at the festival
peace smelled of sentimental saxophone on the wind.
Vendors burned incense like bonfires
and sold "Impeach!" buttons –
but peace has no cousin in pink pamphlets filled
with imploring reproving black exclamation points.
Nothing but additives!!!
                    Peace really
tastes like strong coffee in a styrofoam cup
sipped at the foot of the Rocky Mountains,
feels like turning off the hearing aid,
looks like a small lake rippled by a falling leaf.
Peace is two fat catfish just below the surface
floating on the current, sunning.
Peace is the small green pillow
that smells like the back of her neck,
is watching her rub the creases under her breasts,
both hands, every night the bra drops to our bed,
every night – peace is a beginning
like a fresh deck of cards, like crisp new cotton sheets,
like this morning.
                    I want peace, the sound
of dripping gutters. I want
no history. I want a long red canoe.
I want my sons to stand up straight,
never to pull a trigger. I want
peace that is one infinite moment
gentle as an eyelash.

after the earthquake
the old hotel
stands

POSTCARD FROM IXTAPA

Here we honeymooned – Los Brisos Hotel – view the
same, room the same, private balcony, hammock
perfect for lovemaking.   Pacific waves carried us, tossed
us, filled our swimsuits with sand. I can afford more at
the bar today, order Margaritas at the pool – going
back, back through the dark labyrinth, so many detours
to the sun – face older, body thicker, feet more tired.

pebbles in pocket
pagan rosary

POSTCARD FROM SANTA FE

Driving on Paseo del Perletta, CD player surrounds me with wooden flute – music purchased from the musician's hands at the Taos pueblo. Turn onto Artist Road, elevation 7000 feet, where seashell fossils cover the ground – at Jeanette's home, a meditation crypt, built into the red earth of New Mexico – inside, blue silence, small skylight – improvise flute melodies in my ears – crows cactus earth breathing, high desert wind.

TOURIST

pure
blue sky
wide open two-lane
speeding passed green
and brown plowed fields,
cheap cigar, loud blues music—
old
brown
horse
walks heavily
back
to
his barn
slow
ly
shaking his head

ON GREEN BAY

My oars dip, rouse a lonely ripple –
tiny aluminum rowboat glides
through roaring
silence. The Earth
holds its breath
at 7 am on a Friday in June
so that I
            can listen –
hear the shimmy of minnows.

on the beech leaf
the last raindrop
a sky too big

POSTCARD FROM WASHINGTON ISLAND, WISC.

This sleepy island never rests, waves waves waves –
International Harvester tractors rust in place, tall grass
rising through dry axles, more trees here than wheat or
potatoes – whitefish dinner, light and tender, the
islander waitress, fat and sassy – at Fiddler's Green Pub a
piano sits on the front lawn, still in tune – only the moon
lights the way after 9 pm – this island never wants, there
is enough, 10,000 grandfathers casting nets.

TIME TO GO

Every café closes –
the waiter finishes his last cigarette
tells you politely to pick-up your lousy notebook,

it's time to leave.
Sometimes you stand outside back doors
too long, you become a red-check flannel shirt

hanging limp on a hook –
you're outside the circle of bar jokes
and baptisms and wee-hour

lovemaking. Sometimes it's just time
to go home. Go Jack, to your cats
where Mamere irons your shirts and makes

your highballs. I think it's time –
my grass at home needs cutting, the deck
needs cleaning. I have to go now

put this box of sad souvenirs away in my closet
behind the beat old gym shoes and
silk ties fallen from their plastic hangers.

I miss her warm thigh against my hip.
There is pasticcio baking in the oven.
Roses are blooming over my arbor.

ABOUT THE AUTHOR

Albert DeGenova is a prize-winning poet, editor, teacher, and blues saxophonist. From 1978-1980 he was an editor of the *Oyez Review* (published by Roosevelt University); in June of 2000 he launched the literary/arts journal *After Hours*, for which he continues as publisher and editor. DeGenova received his MFA in Writing from Spalding University, Louisville, and now leads the annual Norbert Blei Writing Workshop at The Clearing Folk School in Ellison Bay, Wisconsin. Other books of poetry by DeGenova include: *Black Pearl* (2016, Purple Flag Press); *A Good Hammer* (2014, a limited edition hand-made letterpress imprint from Timberline Press); *The Blueing Hours* (2008, Virtual Artists Collective); *Back Beat* (2006, Fractal Edge Press, 2nd edition); and *A Tender Spot* (1992, BlueBari Press), DeGenova splits his time between metropolitan Chicago and Sturgeon Bay, WI.

all the planes are silenced
the thunderstorm sings
her wicked, sexy song